Letting Go

Letting Go

REFLECTIONS AND PRAYERS FOR MIDLIFE

Judy Esway

XXIII

TWENTY-THIRD PUBLICATIONS

Mystic, Connecticut

Twenty-Third Publications
185 Willow Street
P.O. Box 180
Mystic, CT 06355
(203) 536-2611

ISBN 0-89622-434-1
Library of Congress Catalog Card Number 90-70622

Dedicated
with all my love to

René Elaine Batson
Valerie Jean Esway
Ricardo Paul Esway

Letting go of you, dear children,
is the most difficult of all.

Contents

Letting Go

Introduction

I FEEL LIKE SINGING "Happy Birthday to me. Happy Birthday to me." Today is my 50th birthday! Oh, I wonder if it's all right for me to sing today. I think I'm supposed to be depressed.

Writing this book has been therapeutic for me. I think that's why I'm not the least bit depressed. It's helped me to come to grips with reality. It forced me to look long and hard at my life and make some choices that needed to be made as I enter into my later years.

One thing is sure, that's where I'm headed. But how will I go? I could go screaming and kicking or I could go willingly, with a sense of adventure. The choice is mine.

I was a person who was always looking forward to the bright future. I can't tell you exactly when it happened but at one point I found myself looking backward, reflecting on all that I had already lived. Little snatches of my past would spring to mind, even back to childhood. Once I found myself a little girl again, kneeling in the grass in our backyard, gazing in wonder at the huge orange sunflowers lining the fence.

Or I was back in the hospital delivery room holding one of our newborns, feeling the same rush of love. Often I'd go back to my father's funeral 10 years earlier and vividly recall every detail.

One day when I was in the middle of a conversation with my 16-year-old daughter, like a flash of light in my mind, she was five years old again. I was taking her to her first day of kindergarten. I could almost smell her freshly pressed dress, blue checkered with a yellow sash tied in a perfect bow around her waist.

This looking back didn't seem to be a conscious thing on my part. Perhaps it's a normal part of human development to come to a place where we must stop and review. I had to assure myself that those years were not wasted, that what I did was important and worthwhile.

I wanted to mark my 50th birthday in a special way, not with a fancy gift or party (although I may change my mind—the day is still young), but with another book. Since the publication of my second book, *Womanprayer/Spirit-journey*, in 1987, I had been unsuccessful at writing another. Even though I felt there was something inside me crying to be said, I couldn't quite hear it. Nothing I wrote felt right. One idea after another ended up as crumpled paper in the trash.

Maybe there was nothing left for me to say. Maybe I had said all that I knew how to say in my last book. Those who know me will laugh at that. Judy? Nothing to say? Never....

Then one day after a long, frustrating period, with my 50th birthday approaching and no book in sight, the phone rang. Pat Kluepfel, Acquisitions Editor for Twenty-Third Publications, was wondering if I might have another book in the works for them. I told Pat my dilemma and we did some brainstorming together.

Pat suggested several things but nothing clicked. We threw out one idea after another until Pat finally said, "How about a book of meditations on letting go?" That was it. I knew it immediately.

That's what I was supposed to write about because that's where I was in my life, trying to let go of so many things. I thanked Pat and went right to work. My writer's block had been broken and the book that had been striving to be born all along poured out of me inside of three months.

Letting go. We all have to do it but some of us have more difficulty with it than others. I'm one of those. I get attached to things, not to material things so much (except for my water bed), but to emotional experiences and to people, oh, Lord, always to people.

This time of life requires a great deal of letting go. As 50 moved closer, I had to grapple with the many subtle changes taking place in my life. My face and body were changing, my hair was getting gray, our children were leaving. I had to face some things. If I were to grow old gracefully and with joy, a certain courage would be needed. I would have to trust God as together we moved down a road I had never walked before.

When I allowed myself to think about aging, the forbidden topic, a new understanding slowly opened up to me. The whole process started to interest me. For instance, I put off coloring my hair (maybe I won't any more) because suddenly I was intrigued at watching it turn gray. And while in the past I could hardly stand to see new lines emerge on my face, they too took on an interesting aspect. It seemed that the more squarely I faced the reality of what was happening, the less fearful I became.

This is a new season of my life. I want it to be spectacular as Autumn was meant to be. The only way that can happen is if I breathe the wonderful crisp air, immerse myself in the dramatic, changing colors, and hug the trees.

This will take a new level of concentration, a letting go of distractions. Spring and summer have passed. I have made my choice. I will live the rest of my days with passion and intensity.

There's a lot of humor in this book. I didn't set out to write a funny book but I'm glad I did. I don't think I could have made it through parenthood, or even life for that matter, without a sense of humor. It would please me to know that perhaps you've chuckled your way through these pages and even shed a few tears. I think you'll do both as you "connect" with your own experience of letting go.

When I started writing this book, I said to a friend, "If I write about all the things I'm struggling to let go of, I might look like I'm totally neurotic."

My friend answered, "Neurotic people are people who refuse to let go, who are so afraid of change they won't even acknowledge their need to let go of anything. Healthy people are always in the struggle of letting go."

I liked that.

This book is about my struggle to let go, to stop looking back, and to move forward. I don't believe we can do this all at once; it's a gradual process. So the things I've written about are in various stages. In some areas I've made beautiful progress; in others I've only just begun.

The more I've been able to let go, the lighter and happier I am. And the lighter I am, the faster I can run through the falling leaves to hug the tree of life. When I embrace the tree, I embrace God and say yes to all God offers me, moment by moment.

You can't hug if your arms are full. You have to drop everything and open your arms wide for a maximum intensity hug....Let go. If I can do it, so can you!

Hormones Don't Discriminate

TALK ABOUT UNCOMFORTABLE. There I was seated in the waiting room of the ob-gyn's office surrounded by young, pregnant women. They were happily thumbing through baby magazines, chatting about due dates and names for their newborns. I kept a low profile, hoping nobody would see I was reading a brochure on menopause.

Later I sat in the young doctor's office as he counseled me about hormones and hot flashes, estrogen and mood swings. I could have laughed at the ridiculous scene if I weren't so close to tears.

Inside I was yelling, *"Stop it. Don't you know how awful it makes me feel to be sitting here talking about menopause? Don't you know that only yesterday I was one of those beautiful, glowing women in your outer office?"*

He droned on, oblivious to my pain. "And some women will have hot flashes, especially during the night. If they become too uncomfortable we can..."

"Blah, blah, blah...you, young...male! What on earth do you know about it! Can't you see I'm just trapped in this aging body? Can't you see who I really am?"

Oh, God, I've never had to get old before. I don't know how to do it, at least not gracefully. I thought I would breeze through the change of life because of my relationship with you. But I soon discovered that hormones don't discriminate. They have no respect for spiritual things.

God, help me to let go of my youth, especially the days when I was a young mother, those beautiful chapters of my life when I felt needed and important. You needed me, God, didn't you? We "created" together. The three of us entered into a joint venture, producing priceless human treasures who will live forever.

Help me now to let it all pass away gently, and please, please let me see the beauty of these final years. You still need me, don't you, God?

Happy Childhood

FINALLY, AFTER 30 YEARS of marriage, Rick and I were going on our first real vacation. A slightly belated 25th-anniversary gift to each other.

As we were making plans, a funny feeling came over me. It felt like guilt, the "useless" emotion. (I'm fond of calling it that, but it's not fooled.) "Rick, we can't go. I don't think we ever took the kids on a long vacation. Did we?"

"Jude, we moved so much they've been all over the country. They've seen more than most kids."

"Does that count?" I picked up the phone to call our married daughter in San Diego. "René, do you remember if we went on family vacations when you were little?"

"Of course. I have good memories of vacation time; we went almost every year. Don't tell me you forgot that, too, Mom."

I guess I was relieved but I called our college student in Flagstaff, just in case.

"Valerie, did we go on many vacations when you were little?"

She hesitated. "Huh? Yea, I guess. I don't know."

"I knew it."

"Mom, don't worry about it. I'm not scarred. Honest."

"Are you sure?"

"Mom, I keep telling you I had a happy childhood. Trust me. I wouldn't lie about a thing like that."

"René said we took you kids to Disneyland and the Grand Canyon and..."

"Oh, yea, we did. Sure we did. Will you and Dad just go to Hawaii and have a good time!"

Our high school freshman overheard us. "Ricky, Dad and I were thinking maybe we'd postpone our Hawaii trip and we'll all go on a family..."

"No, no. I knew this was coming. Don't say it. Not a family vacation. I'm not leaving my friends for a whole week. Count me out."

Well, at least I didn't have to worry about him.

I saw the son of a famous comedian on a television talk show a while back. He chuckled as he related childhood stories. "When Dad tucked me in bed at night he'd whisper in my ear, 'Ronnie, you're having a happy childhood. You're having a happy childhood.'"

I wish I had thought of doing that, God. I've tried so hard over the years to protect the children, to keep their delicate little psyches healthy. And even now when they're grown, I'm still fretting about the past, wishing I had done this or hadn't done that. Please help me to let go of my need to be a perfect parent when I know full well there is no such thing.

Please heal our children of any problems they may experience because we weren't perfect, only human. And, God, help them to know, deep down where it counts, how much they were wanted and cherished.

Just Don't!

GOD, WHY CAN'T I RELAX? Why do I always have to be productive? Why can't I just be?

Forgive me, God, but sometimes I think you might be somewhat responsible for my dilemma. It was you that gave me so many interests. You made the world so rich and full of things that fascinate me. You made life with endless layers and you made me a person who is never satisfied merely skimming the surface. I dive in, exhilarated, drawn by the wonder and beauty of life in the deep. But when I emerge, I'm exhausted and frustrated.

I said to Rick one evening, "Life was so much simpler when I didn't want to read everything and explore every avenue and form deep friendships with everyone in the world and..." He listened to me, contentedly stirring the bubbly, red spaghetti sauce he was preparing for dinner. When I finished, he put down the spoon, took my face in his hands and said quietly, "Then don't."

"What do you mean, just like that? Just don't?"

"Just like that. Just don't."

He lifted the wooden spoon to my mouth. "Taste. Good, huh?"

God, help me to "just don't." Help me to change my mind-set from "produce, grow, develop, learn" to "slow down, relax, tomorrow's another day."

I don't like to admit it but sometimes this attitude will even enter my prayer. What an absurd contradiction, when in recent years my contemplative side has blossomed. I can spend hours "wasting time" with you, God, resting in your delicious presence. But secretly (as if I can keep a secret from you, God), I find myself measuring the productivity of my wasted time. The longer I do nothing, I reason, the more I'll accomplish in prayer. God, this is getting complicated.

Help me to realize that no matter how much I try, I'll never be able to satisfy this need to see how far I can go. And I'll never be able to fill this deepening canyon of curiosity you've placed inside me. Help me to trust that you will fill it completely some day, at some other level of consciousness. After all, God, I don't think you'd want it to go to waste!

Time Tunnel

THIS WAS THE YEAR of our 30th wedding anniversary and my 50th birthday and I was having problems. Oh, not so anyone could tell (I was careful about that), but I knew I was stuck in some uncomfortable place in time. I couldn't go forward and I longed to go back. Not a very healthy situation.

I wanted to revisit my life, just once. If I could only find a time tunnel to slip down into and come back when I was ready. (I certainly wouldn't want to stay!) Looking at old photo albums, trying to remember when the children were young seemed to help some, but not enough to make me move.

Rummaging around in the garage one day I came across a box of forgotten, dusty reels of tape, old home movies. I decided to take them to a camera store and have them transferred to a video. Maybe I had found my time tunnel.

Our life was now neatly contained in a two-hour video and I was happy to be home alone for the first viewing. I fumbled around with the VCR, excited about the treasure I held in my hands. Aaaahh...success. Words splashed across the screen, "Rick and Judy Esway—Family Memories."

"Easy listening" music had been added; the melancholy strains hastened my nostalgia attack. It had been years since we showed any of these films.

A flash of white, a $79 wedding gown and a borrowed veil with a tiara top, appeared first. My eyes filled with tears when the young bride in the size 7 gown twirled around the dance floor with her handsome husband. Then she was a young mother holding her babies close. I watched in amazement as another woman with grace and confidence slowly emerged. I relived parties and picnics as the children grew taller. They laughed and blew out birthday candles and clowned for the cameraman they adored. For two hours, I ooohed and aaahed and ached all over as I watched my life flash before me.

It didn't matter that my husband had turned the camera sideways once, I just turned my head to compensate. It didn't even matter that most of the bodies were headless. After all, a mother knows her children. And so I felt a little motion sickness when Rick panned the camera back and forth as blurred figures threw a ball to each other. It didn't matter. Nothing was going to spoil my trip down memory lane.

The next morning I awoke early, feeling emotional, images from another lifetime still swirling through my head. I shook my sleeping husband. "I watched the video last night. Did you know that no one in our family has a head?"

He mumbled. "What on earth are you talking about?"

"The video. Our home movies. Thirty years of our lives and you cut off everyone's head."

He opened one eye to look at the clock. "Honey, you wake me at 5:00 A.M. to tell me I'm a lousy cameraman?"

"And there's not one picture of Ricky, our only son, our baby, in the whole two hours!"

"Nobody has a picture of their youngest child."

"What are we going to tell him?"

"Maybe he won't notice."

That evening we watched the film together. To our fourteen year old it must have looked ancient. Ricky said quite seriously, "Did they colorize it?" I had to stop and think. "No, it's not that old! How old do you think we are anyhow?"

"Old." (I think he was teasing.) "What's that music? Sick."

I smiled. "Oh, life came with music in those days. Everything was so wonderful then."

"Sure, Mom. What happened to the heads? You took these, didn't you, Dad?"

"Well..."

I saved him. "Look, look at René. She was 12 days old there. We had her first picture taken that day. Remember?" I thought Rick looked a little funny.

"Look at that," he said. "There's my '57 Chevy. I should have kept it."

I looked a little funny.

"There's Valerie with her arm in a cast. Remember when she broke her arm? Poor baby. That must have been in 1971."

"Couldn't have been. There's my Olds. I didn't have it in '71. I loved that car. Remember that hot orange interior?"

"Where am I?" Ricky asked.

Rick cleared his throat. "You weren't born yet."

"There's René at her first communion. Oh, look how beautiful she looked. That must have been in, let's see, she was born in '63 so this must have been in '70."

"Wrong again. There's my Merc. I didn't get that until '72."

"Shhh..." I leaned forward. "Look at Valerie. She's got that big bruise on her nose. Remember when she fell flat on her face and her nose was one big bruise? It was awful. Remember?"

Rick looked funny again. I was getting peeved. "You're not going to tell me you don't remember that bruise on Val's nose, are you?"

"Where am I?" Ricky piped in.

Rick cleared his throat again. "You weren't born yet, son."

"I can't believe this. You remember every stupid car you ever had but you don't remember that bruise on your daughter's nose?"

"Judy, I can't believe you expect me to remember a bruise on a kid's nose from 30 years ago!"

"Twenty. How could you forget?"

Ricky stood up to leave the room. "Maybe I was adopted."

"Wait, son," Rick said. "There you are."

Our son glanced over his shoulder. "No head," he muttered and kept walking. "This is boring."

I whispered, "You know that wasn't him. You lied!"

"You'll never be able to prove that."

"I could if I could see his head!"

Rick smiled. "I know...."

Let's Be Friends

GOD, PLEASE HELP ME to let go of potential friendships that never materialize and help me to be mature when my offer of friendship is turned down. (I know you're smiling, God.) So I act a little childish when I'm rejected. Doesn't everybody?

When someone lets me know they're not interested in pursuing a closer relationship ("Nothing personal; it's not you," they explain), I act calm and dignified. "No problem," I say. "I understand perfectly. It's my loss."

But inside I think, "Are you crazy? It's really your loss. Do you know what a great friend I am? Do you want references or something? Do you need a resume?"

Well, God, I guess there's someone else who knows how I handle, or don't handle, rejection. What would I do without my understanding husband? He lets me vent all my emotions, no matter how long it takes, and never flinches or raises an eyebrow. "

"Jude," he says, "it could be that some people are a little frightened by your openness. Not everyone can handle intimacy like you. And let's face it, you don't waste time. You've always been that way. You meet someone and you say, 'Boom, I like you. Let's be friends. What did you say your name was?'"

"I don't say 'Boom,'" I laughed, "and I always make a point of getting their name first."

"Hon, you are a wonderful friend to have and it is their loss but you have to accept it, not everybody is into friendship like you are. You've practically made a career out of it."

"Lucky for you," I answered. "Look how many interesting people I've brought home."

God, doesn't everybody know that's what heaven is all about? Friendship with you and all those fascinating people you've created. I'm just practicing, that's all. I feel better. I don't think I have time for another friend right now anyway. But tell me, God, there's no such thing as rejection in heaven, is there?

Making Ends Meet

GOD, PLEASE HELP ME to let go of my need for financial security. I know I worry too much about money, but all the years we were raising our family we couldn't save a dime. Even now our expenses are high with a big house payment, a daughter in college and a son soon to follow. And the years left for us to work are numbered.

So many fears plague me. What if we lose our jobs? What if one of us gets sick? What if we have to go to a nursing home? Every time I get overly "what if'd," Lord, you show me the same Scripture. "Take the lilies: they do not spin, they do not weave; but I tell you, Solomon in all his splendor was not arrayed like any one of them. If God clothes in such splendor the grass of the field, which grows today and is thrown on the fire tomorrow, how much more will he provide for you, O weak in faith!" (Luke 12:27, 28)

Sometimes, God, when you're not looking, I'm so tempted to just lift that page right out of my Bible.

Forgive me when I worry, God. You have proven over and over that you do take care of us. And as we've grown bolder in charitable works, your blessings have come in countless ways.

"...Your Father knows that you need such things. Seek out instead his kingship over you, and the rest will follow in turn." (Luke 12:30–31)

Whenever I worry, God, remind me of all the times you've surprised us and met our needs in the most unlikely manner. An unexpected check arrives just in the nick of time, a friend pays a long-forgotten debt, a refund arrives on something that we had long forgotten about.

Help me to seek out your kingship in my life, God. Help me to stop expending so much energy trying to spin and weave a flimsy web of security when I have the greatest security of all—in my loving God.

Letters After My Name

GOD, HELP ME TO LET GO of my dreams, at least the ones that have no hope of coming true any more. There were so many roads I'd wanted to walk down; each alone would have taken a lifetime.

It's too late now to be a concert pianist, or a dancer, or a Ph.D—in anything. I don't care what. I just want some letters after my name. I've always been envious of people with letters after their name. My nun friend, Sr. Lois, had O.P., B.S., and M.A.T after hers. And she just graduated with a second masters degree (as if one weren't enough). Now she gets to add M.A.L.S. How's she going to get anything done now, God? It will take her fifteen minutes to sign her name!

Is that fair? How can I get some letters? I mean without becoming a nun, or giving up my job to devote precious years to intense study. Can't I just get a couple of little letters, like honorary or something?

I dreamed of becoming a Renaissance Woman (I think I just like saying it), but I've only learned a little bit about a lot of things, just enough to make me dangerous, as the old saying goes. I haven't become an expert in anything. Wait... Maybe I've learned a lot about life. That's it, God. I've been an avid student and keen observer of life. And I've spent years learning the art of love. Are there university degrees in Life and Love 101?

Help me to let go of my dreams, God, and to be satisfied with what I have accomplished in my life. Maybe I was right where you wanted me to be, doing exactly what you hoped I would.

So then, God, do you think when I get to heaven you might possibly have a few leftover letters to add to my name? How about Judy Esway, M.Lv. (Master of Love)?

Something Must Be Wrong

GOD, HELP ME TO LET GO of this nagging feeling I always get when things are going well. I have such an exciting job right now and maybe I think I don't deserve it. Or if I do deserve it, then it should at least have the decency to be boring sometimes. And if not boring, then the people I work with should be dull or difficult.

As legal secretary to the in-house counsel for a high-tech corporation, none of the above is true. The computer software company we work for employs people who are smart, witty, and stimulating to be around. Norm, my boss, is wonderful (I guess he hasn't heard how attorneys are supposed to be). He and I are the "Legal Department."

Working for Norm is like living on the edge of a cliff. We file court pleadings within minutes of the deadline. We save clients from impending doom, translate mountains of legal gibberish, and close important deals always at the last possible minute. After endless revisions we pull papers out of the laser printer and throw them into Norm's briefcase as he's running late (Norm's always running late) to a big meeting.

"Judy, would you call..." I finish his sentence and pick up the phone "...and tell them you've been unavoidably detained—again—and you'll be a little late."

"Don't say 'again,'" he laughs, and dashes out the door.

I asked him once, "Norm, tell me why we always have to go through these cliff-hangers. Why can't we get ready early, just once?"

He placed his hands on my shoulders and charmed me again with his boyish grin. "Judy, it wouldn't be any fun that way."

God, I love to get up and go to work in the morning. I even sing in the car. (I hope I'm not a masochist.) But after all these years in the workplace I think I've finally found the perfect position. So why do I worry that something will happen?

"We're a team," Norm says. "We perform miracles together." God, it's wonderful being part of a team instead of simply being an employee. And when that kind of chemistry and attitude is present, people can perform miracles.

Thank you for my job, God. Don't let me spoil it by worrying that something will spoil it. And help me when I feel like I can't go through one more panic to remember that living on the edge of a cliff can keep you very, very alert!

Spring Cleaning

MY HEART IS CLUTTERED, God. And so are my "special" drawers and boxes and little hiding places. They're bulging with letters and pictures and "things" that hold lovely, bittersweet memories.

How can I let the treasure of my life go? Can I just whisk it all up in my arms and throw it into the trash? I can't let it go. These things are too precious to me. Yet, I know I must do something. I must make way for the "now," for the present-day experience that will soon enough be tomorrow's memory.

How often I find myself looking at the wave long after it has passed me when the new wave takes me by surprise. I didn't see it coming. I was still remembering and yearning for the last experience, the best wave, or so I thought. But each wave you bring me, God, is the best wave. Each one fresh and exhilarating.

I'm trying, you know I am, to experience life as a fantastic piece of music. I don't want to stay too long with a note that's meant to be a staccato, even when it jabs my soul and makes me bleed. I need to move on with the music and flow and dance with it. But you know how I tend to linger too long, not trusting that the next measure will touch and embrace me as much as the last.

Help me, God, to unclutter my heart. Give me a thorough spring cleaning and rearrange me any way you like. God, how I need fresh air and room to breathe. I want to be empty so I can feel the new wave washing over me. I want to be refreshed and ready to listen with my whole heart to the new song filling my soul.

I Used to Cook...Honest

GOD, I LOVE BEING a modern woman living in an age where women have more options. And men, too, for that matter. And I'm grateful that I'm married to a man who's not a chauvinist. Traditional roles have not been ours for some time now. The children have seen their father in the kitchen more than their mother in recent years. It's great, honest it is, to be liberated and have more time to pursue other interests.

So why do I feel guilty at times? I knew Rick was only kidding when he said last month, "What are you kids getting me for Mothers Day?"

I should be happy and I am. At first when Rick started invading "my" kitchen I found it annoying. He was interested when I decided to learn how to make all the wonderful meals his mother had made so we could pass our Italian tradition on to our children. Rick loved the idea and kept showing up in the kitchen, watching over my shoulder, saying things like "I don't think Mom did it that way. You didn't put enough garlic in that. Jude, let me do this part. I don't think you've got it quite right." He really got on my nerves after a while until one day I walked out of the kitchen and never went back (except to eat).

But that was after 20 years of cooking and cleaning and baking and being the best Suzie Homemaker in the world. I don't think I feel guilty, God, but just a little upset because the kids hardly remember those years.

Rick turned out to be a wonderful cook. And he knows I taught him everything but when he gets all the praise, does he ever mention that little critical piece of information? I guess I shouldn't really complain because when he first started cooking I felt a wonderful freedom. I knew a good thing when I saw it coming so I started praising him first, especially in front of people. I'm not stupid!

I know I overreacted that Sunday, God, when we were all at the dinner table. The children, our new son-in-law, and some friends were over, and Rick outdid himself. He cooked a three-course Italian meal and served everyone, fussing and filling wine glasses, tending to everyone's needs. Then the praises filled the room—ooooohhhs and aaaaahhhs and uuuuummmms—and Rick smiled humbly and said, "Are you sure it's good? I'm not too sure" (a ploy for more praise).

"Oh, yes, it's great!" one said. Another, "Fantastic. The homemade noodles melt in your mouth." Our company chimed in, "I've never tasted Italian food like this in my life."

Suddenly I got jealous. It came out of nowhere as jealousy usually does. I had to say something and I couldn't even wait until they stopped talking. I blurted it out. "Do you kids remember when I used to cook?"

The whole table grew silent. Everyone looked at me, forks poised in mid-air. No one answered. They just resumed eating and talking.

It made me even more irrational. I said it again, only louder. "Don't you kids remember when I used to cook?"

They all looked at me, then at each other.

René, our married daughter, spoke up first. "I remember,

Mom. You used to make us real good breakfasts when we were little. That's right. Now I remember."

Valerie was 16 at the time. She patted my hand consolingly. "It's okay, Mom. If you say you cooked, we believe you."

Ricky was 11. He looked surprised. "You used to cook?"

That did it, God. I didn't care, company or not. I blew up and stormed out of the dining room. "Twenty years I cooked for you kids and cleaned and did everything for you —everything! Twenty years, and you only remember what Dad did?"

God, we laugh about that day now but I still feel a twinge of jealousy. Help me to let go of it. I like the freedom of not having to do everything myself. I want Rick to cook (I just wish he weren't so good at it). But I admit I do still feel a little guilty that I'm not in the kitchen "where women are supposed to be."

Help me, God, to give up this nonsense. Help me to let go of the guilt and enjoy the pasta!

Security Blanket

GOD, SO MANY OF my old devotions have slipped away from me. They just don't seem to fit any more. All I want to do is read your Word, talk to you like a friend, then slip down into silence. I hear myself breathe... in and out... slowly, deeply. It's all I want. You're all I want.

But, God, I don't want to let go of my old devotions completely. They're so much a part of my religious identity and I still need them from time to time. When a friend of mine was in terrible trouble, for three days I prayed every prayer I ever knew. I was too nervous and anxious for my friend to sit in silent prayer, yet I had to do something.

Like a hurt child searching through her room for a security blanket, I found myself rummaging through drawers, pulling out faded holy cards, forgotten prayer books, broken rosaries, and bottles of holy water. I fasted and cried and prayed to saints who made bold promises in exchange for a few simple prayers. I was desperate and had to return to earlier days.

Lord, thank you for all that suited me as I grew and developed in prayer. But help me not to feel guilty when most of the time those former devotions don't wear well. Only in silence do I find you, God. Only in the breathing and the beating of our hearts.

A Changing Church

I DON'T UNDERSTAND ME, God. I hope you do. How often I'm upset with the church for not moving faster, yet I still hang on to old memories.

Catholic grade school. I was always happy when it was time for Forty Hours Procession. Alone in my room, I looked in the mirror and fantasized. In my white dress and long white veil, I imagined I was an angel on a very special mission. I was to carry flowers and prepare a fragrant way for Jesus.

I joined other little girls dressed in white waiting at the front of the church. I held my wicker basket of flowers carefully. Now it was time. We walked slowly into the church, like Sister said, down the long white runner in the center aisle. I picked a bright red rose from my basket, peeled it, and dropped one petal at a time. Each tiny spot of velvet looked alive as it floated mystically to sweeten Jesus' path.

A long line of priests, two by two, young and old, followed the angels in white taffeta, satin, and net. Processing around the church, up and down each aisle, their praising voices boomed in deep, baritone sounds. *Pange lingua gloriosi, corporis mysterium.*

I can still smell the incense and hear the sound of the chain hanging from the monstrance the priest carried that held the sacred host. "Clink... clink... clink..." Old women with black lace doilies on their heads made the sign of the cross as Jesus passed by. Then their fingers returned to the ever-present rosary beads looped around their hands.

As I grew older I looked forward to the Novenas to the Blessed Mother. "Hail, Holy Queen, Mother of Mercy... Hail Mary, full of grace... Lovely lady dressed in blue, teach me how to pray. God was just your little boy; tell me what to say."

And the mysterious benediction. *Tantum ergo, sacramentum*... Blessed be God, Blessed be His holy name, Blessed be God in His angels and in His saints."

Ah, the Baltimore Catechism. Sister would teach us every other subject but we had to wait for Father to come to our classroom to teach us about God. (I guess nuns couldn't do anything that important. They were women.)

"Why did God make us?" Father would ask. He answered his own question. "To know Him, to love Him, and to serve Him." I remember how surprised and excited I felt the first time I heard those words. I almost jumped up and said, "Oh, wow... we get to know God!"

I waited and waited to meet God. I daydreamed about what I should say. "Hello, God. I'm Judy. Oh, well, I guess you already knew that." I wanted to be ready because surely one day soon Father would bring God with him. After all, he couldn't expect me to love God and serve Him when I didn't even know Him.

Father never brought God with him so I started to look for other people who might introduce me to God. I thought Patty and Guy probably knew God. They were just little kids like me but they were so holy. At Mass, they went to Communion every single morning and they kind of glowed.

I wanted to go to Communion every morning, too, but the rule was you couldn't eat or drink anything from midnight the night before until after you received Communion, and I was always starving as soon as I opened my eyes. Patty and Guy were the only ones in the whole classroom holy enough to do that. Then they got to eat egg salad sandwiches and drink chocolate milk at their desks while the rest of us weak, full sinners had to listen to Sister Naomi teach English. Patty and Guy didn't even have to open their books. They just sat there with light all around them, eating egg salad sandwiches.

For a long time I hoped they would introduce me to God, but it became pretty clear that they planned to keep God to themselves. Funny, but I always thought Sister liked them more than us, except one time she got mad at Guy who was the holiest altar boy also.

One morning after Guy served at Mass, he pointed out to Father that Father had made a mistake during Mass and Sister found out about it and she really yelled at Guy. Poor Guy. Could he help it he was so smart?

I finally made it to 8th grade and could participate in the May crowning. Patty, of course, was the May Queen. We all knew we didn't stand a chance. The holiest person got to crown Mary by gently placing the garland of flowers on the statue's head. I would have been too nervous for that anyway. But my best friend, Phyllis, and I talked to Sister Matilda and told her that we had a meeting and all of us girls had planned the celebration. Patty would be the Queen and Phyllis and I would be the attendants. The other five girls in the 8th grade would just have to settle for being in the procession. Not very democratic, I know, but Sister said okay as long as everyone agreed. We sort of let her think everyone agreed. Well, they did, after we promised them they could wear long gowns too, but not blue.

It was May. The long-awaited magical day had finally arrived. Patty was dressed in a billowy white wedding gown and Phyllis and I wore long blue gowns—Mary's color—and I swear Mary looked alive when Patty placed the flowers on her head and we sang "On this day, oh, beautiful Mother, on this day, we give you our love."

Oh, God, how precious it all was. But as much as I miss those days, I don't want the church to go back. We need to change and mature and evolve.

Help me to place the memories in the proper place and to let go of the nagging feeling I have that something wonderful has been lost. Help me to look for the new beauty that comes from a church struggling for maturity.

And please, God, help me to let go of the ingrained sense of guilt and unworthiness that was hammered into me all those years. Help me to forgive a church that is finally trying to own up to its mistakes—a church I'll always love.

So Don't Listen!

GOD, WHY IS IT that children resist taking advice from their parents? We could save them so much trouble and grief if they would just listen! We've made every mistake imaginable and we'd love to have them benefit from what we had to learn the hard way. We just want to make life easier for them.

Mostly, we try to bite our tongues but sometimes we can't resist trying to warn them. "Don't run up your charge accounts. You can't imagine how quickly they can get out of hand."

"I know, I know," they smile sweetly, humoring us.

"We don't want to tell you how to run your life but Dad and I joined exercise spas dozens of times since we've been married and for as often as we used them we figure each visit cost us $300."

"I know, Mom, but I'm different. I'm going to go twice a day. You'll see."

"Do you really need a brand new car? How are you ever going to make that payment?"

"Oh, you just watch. I have it all figured out."

After one of these conversations, Rick and I brooded

alone. "They're going to do it," he said. "They're going to totally mess up their lives."

"I know. Oh, why won't they listen? Why won't they benefit from our mistakes?" We looked at each other and at the same knowing moment burst into laughter. Had we benefited from anyone else's mistakes? We must not have or we wouldn't have gotten into so much trouble over the years.

Help us, God, to allow our children to live their own lives and figure things out on their own. I'm starting to think it's terribly wrong to take away another person's problems, almost like stealing.

I have a friend who refuses to let me have a problem. When I tell her of one, she instantly solves it for me. If only I do what she says—this, that, and such and such—presto! my problem will vanish. I didn't know why it bothered me so much until one day I realized I didn't want anyone to take away my problems. They're mine and mine alone to solve.

Help me to remember this, God, when I'm tempted to "help" our children. Let me love them enough to allow them to make their own mistakes and solve their own problems. Help me to resist rushing in too soon—but help me also to know when I should.

Grandma? Who, Me?

IT'S SO WONDERFUL having grandchildren, God. Thank you for blessing us with three precious little girls to love. Angela, Caitlin, and Emily have changed the personality of our family. We're richer now.

I think I'm going to be a good grandmother, God, surprise...surprise. At first I couldn't even say the word, at least not in connection with me. I tried so hard with Angela to say, "Come on, baby. Come to Grr.. Grrran.. Grrrandma...." I thought I would choke on the word. You know how I love those three little girls, God, but it's just that word and me. How did I ever get to this place? A grandmother!

I think I suffered a little identity crisis (again) today. René called from San Diego. "Mom, I wanted to tell you something funny. I was reading Angela a story and the book had a picture of a grandmother rocking a baby. The grandma was plump and soft looking and her white hair was pulled back in a bun. And she had just baked a cherry pie that was sitting on the counter cooling. It was funny, Mom. Grandmothers just aren't like that any more. My girls are never going to know a Grandma like that."

"Well, honey. Gosh. I'll be a good grandmother, honest. How about a frozen pie? I don't think Angela will know the difference."

"No, no, Mom. You know I'm proud of you. It's just a little strange, that's all. The girls won't ever know a Grandma like I did. Grandma Esway was just like that Grandma in the book."

"Well, uh, what should I do about it?"

"Nothing, Mom. It's just kind of funny, that's all."

God, why do I feel guilty that I'm not plump and that I don't have white hair pulled back in a bun and I haven't baked a pie in years? But I do sing to our granddaughters and hold them close and love them with as much passion as any grandmother could.

God, I think love is all that matters. I know it is. Help me to forget stereotypes and concentrate on showering our babies with love.

The "Gasp" Class

THEY CALL IT "Beyond Basic Bible." I call it the "Gasp Class." The priests, nuns, and lay people are called teachers. I call them "Illusion Busters."

I've taken classes for years at the Kino Institute in Phoenix, a school of religious studies. But never have I been so challenged and stimulated as I have in this particular class. Once a week for two hours I find myself alternating between tensing all my muscles, gasping, or holding my breath altogether.

"We want you to become mature Christians," they explain. "Now, don't forget, John was writing to his community and addressing the special problems they were experiencing.... You must remember they wrote in a certain literary style that we find difficult to grasp today. We've lost the art of understanding the imagery and symbolic language that was a common expression of their writing."

God, as painful as it is, help me to grow in my understanding of Scripture. Help me to let go of my old concepts, my rigid view of your Word. I want to have a truer insight into what the Bible writers meant to convey. I want to get into their world and into their heads so I can better appreciate the riches of your Word.

It's not easy to do, God. I keep coming at Scripture through my culture, through my time, through my personal history and my eyes as a woman. Help me to be open and allow your holy words to seep into me, down through my bones, to my innermost being. Help me not to judge or restrict their power in any way, for then it will surely change me.

Thank you for your gift of Scripture, God. May I always respect it. May I never abuse it by manipulating it to suit my needs, to control others, or to back up an argument.

And help me to let go of my anxiety of what I might learn next that could upset my little world. In fact, God, feel free to upset it, because each time you have I've discovered a larger world with bright, new treasures to uncover.

A Message From Myself

IT WAS JUNE 1957. I felt relieved and a little tingly that I had made it. I adjusted my cap again and smoothed my gown as I waited in a long line of high school students for the music to begin.

I shivered when the graduation march, that traditional haunting melody, rose up majestically to fill the halls. It signaled us to move, not only into the auditorium where we would receive our diplomas, but into "life" in the scary, real world.

I must have been a reflective person even then, God, because I remember slowly looking around at my classmates—indelibly marking the moment in my mind.

Something unusual happened in those few minutes. I had an instinctive sense that someday I would be looking back at that time of my life with a certain sadness. I knew that as an older woman I might perhaps tend to color that time of my life and wish I were still young. I might be tempted to say (as I've heard so many times since) that those four years were the best years of my life.

It's still a mysterious thing to me, God, but at 17 years old, standing in a hallway at Timken High School in Canton, Ohio, time seemed to lose its meaning. I did something strange. In my head and with all my might, I spoke a clear message to an older woman, a woman who had not yet been formed. The woman was the older me, the woman I am today.

I said with authority, "Judy, don't feel sad that these years are past. Don't remember them as being so fantastic. They were really not all that great. They were just okay, so don't remember them like it's a big loss that they're over."

Now that I'm 50, Lord, I realize what a remarkable thing that was. You've given us some built-in mechanism that "knows." The young me was so right. Those were not the best years of my life. Each year that I grew in maturity and wisdom have been the best years.

But now, God, I'm facing another time of my life that requires insight, courage, and perhaps another message. I don't want to get old. I don't know what to expect. I need to have a message in reverse this time. The Judy who is an old woman needs to speak to me now and tell me I'll be all right. I need to know if I'll still be loved and caressed, valued and respected.

So many elderly people are never touched and never told they're beautiful. No one looks into their eyes. No one satisfies their soul hunger. How many people live alone with little human contact who once lived lives of passion and fire?

Please, God, help me to let go of this terrible fear. Please promise that you'll always provide a means for me to express the powerful feelings inside of me, because they're not diminishing with age but only growing stronger. Oh, God, what shall I do with them?

Only in God

GOD, HOW I NEED to relearn this lesson, time and again. Only you can satisfy my hungry heart. I connect with someone, a soul friend, and I cannot let go. The peak moment ends but not for me. It triggers deep mysterious yearnings, an aching for things of the Spirit.

Sometimes it happens in ordinary conversation with someone I don't even know very well. What is it, God? Do you dance around me? Does the divine spark that lives in each of us suddenly flicker and rise up to touch my heart? That's what it feels like — a flash of fire that melts me and moves me to love.

But I get confused. I want to move closer to that person. Or I'll call another friend hoping they can calm me and spread ointment on my wound. And too often I've placed unrealistic expectations on my husband and others in my life.

When I can find no solace I go into prayer, deep silence, and there I find my soothing balm. It was you, God, that I had wanted all along. It's you that I long for, you that I search for in human relationships even when I know they can never fully satisfy me. "Only in God is my soul at rest."

Help me to let go of people, God, to enjoy them, yes, but not to cling, not to drive them away because I expect them to give me what only you can give.

But please keep dancing around me. I don't mind playing hide and seek with you, God, if it means I can catch a glimpse of you now and then. I need to be assured of your presence until that great day, my last day on earth, when the arms reaching out to me will finally be yours.

That Next Step

GOD, WHEN WILL I ever have the courage to take that next step, the one I've sensed for so long that you're asking me to take? To do my part, to do something—anything—to help the homeless.

The people I see on the street holding signs that read, "Will work for food," provoke disturbing emotions in me. I'm angry at the government, at the churches, at the bureaucracy, at me.

Jesus' haunting words come to me. "The poor, the poor. Don't turn your back on the poor."

I excuse myself in a hundred ways. "You visit the sick. You give money to the homeless shelter and to other charities," etc. But I know in my heart I take the easy way out, the safe way.

But since I met him face to face—a homeless man with a hole in his throat—the time for excuses is over.

It's kind of silly how it came about. I had gone downtown to hear a friend speak at a conference in a plush hotel. I parked my car in a parking garage. Anxious to visit with my friend for a few minutes before she spoke, I took off running without noting where I had parked my car.

Afterwards, I stood on the corner and counted five parking garages within my view and had no idea which one my car was in. Feeling stupid and with my feet hurting, I trudged through three scary garages, and was totally confused. I had to give up.

So there I was. Downtown, alone, and it was getting dark. I swallowed my pride and called home. I related my predicament to our oldest daughter. "You what? Only you, Mom. Dad, Mom lost her car. I'm only telling you what she said."

As I paced back and forth in front of the ritzy hotel waiting for Rick, a strange thing happened. Now when I think of it, it is still somewhat dreamlike, the same as that night.

Limousines pulled in and out of the hotel driveway, transporting well-dressed guests. In striking contrast, impoverished, destitute people were walking on the same block.

A middle-aged man pushed an old woman in a wheelchair that carried all her earthly belongings stuffed in bags. They wore tattered, dirty clothes. Their faces were gaunt. They moved slowly along the side street, near the long, sleek limo that had just pulled to the curb.

A chauffeur dressed in black got out, walked around the man and the woman in the wheelchair as if he didn't see them, to hold the door for the elegant, laughing people stepping out of the white limo. The group walked right past the man and the old woman, never looking at them.

It didn't fit. Something was very wrong. Two separate worlds of human beings, made of the same flesh and blood, breathing the same air, yet seemingly invisible to one another.

I closed my eyes. The scene was all too powerful. Was I the only who could see both worlds? Was my mind playing tricks on me?

An old man, tall and thin, limped slowly toward me. He

had long, gray hair and a gray beard. I backed up, moving closer to the hotel and safety. The man painfully made his way in front of me and sat down on a concrete stoop, next to another limo. He put his face in his hands and moaned lightly. The sound made me feel a terrible loneliness. I had to speak to him.

Quietly, I took a few steps toward him and said, "How are you tonight?" What an unbelievably stupid question!

He looked up at me, a little startled. He had large, soulful eyes.

"Have you eaten anything today?"

He pointed to a hole in his throat, a recent surgery, it seemed, that was still healing. He shook his head and touched his mouth.

"I'm sorry. Are you trying to tell me you can't speak?" I pulled out the seven dollars I had in my wallet and searched through the bottom of my purse. "Here," I closed his hand over the money. "I'm sorry. It's all I have."

He stood up. His sad, blue eyes filled with tears. He kept pointing to his throat, and then his mouth.

People were beginning to look at us now. The worlds had come together. "I'm sorry," I said. "God bless you. I'm so sorry."

I had never been so sorry in my life, sorry he was an old man with no place to lay his head, sorry I was wearing an expensive dress and he was in rags, sorry that I lacked the courage to be the kind of Christian I truly wanted to be.

We walked together to the corner. He crossed his hands over his heart and his eyes grew tender.

My husband drove up. I gave the old man a tissue to wipe his tears. "Goodbye," I said. "I'll never forget you."

There was something familiar about his eyes. He never took them off mine as we held our hands together for a moment. "I promise I will never forget you."

I was silent on the drive home. Rick teased me about losing my car. When I didn't laugh, he said, "What's wrong, honey? Did that old man disturb you?"

"Yes, in the worst way," I answered quietly. "I think that old man was Jesus."

God, give me the courage to take that next step.

Past Hurts

GOD, HELP ME TO let go of past hurts. When-
ever I think things are buried for good, something happens
and memories surface again.

I try to be understanding and to be a person who forgives
easily. I'm painfully aware of how many times I've hurt
others, God, and grateful for the many times I've been
forgiven. Yet, each time I get hurt, I make a mental list of
grievances I have against that person, things I was sure I
had already dealt with.

And after I list those grievances, it triggers other memories of numerous people way back to childhood who have
hurt me over the years and I go on a "poor me" trip that
could last for days.

When I'm exhausted by this, God, I then return to sanity,
recognizing that people are all the same. We're fragile and
we all have super-sensitive feelings. We're always hurting
each other and trying to forgive one another and trying to
get over something. None of us are perfect and we all know
it, yet we still expect perfection in each other.

Help me with this latest hurt which may mean the end of
a long-term special friendship. God, I don't want it to end

but something is wrong with it. It needs a radical change. Too many things went unsaid and were pushed down for years until the inevitable happened. An explosion over something small, all out of proportion to the little, tiny straw that could find no place to land.

Where do we go from here? Do we apologize and try to forget it ever happened? Or do all those buried hurts on both sides need to be expressed? Either way will have its risks and only you, God, know which way is best. Why, oh, why are relationships so difficult? I can understand why most people prefer to keep things superficial and safe. But I can't be that way, God, even though sometimes it's tempting.

Help me in all my relationships. Help me to give up past hurts once and for all. And, God, teach me how to forgive, seventy times seven times seven...as you do with me.

Going to Church

ANOTHER SUNDAY MORNING. Another battle to get our last teenager to go to church with us. God, give me strength to get through this. Give me a sense of humor to pull it off one last time.

God, you know I love our children. They're wonderful people and I'm proud of the three of them. And I know they love me, but something peculiar happens when they reach a certain age. And it only seems to affect them on Sunday mornings. They become vicious. They turn on me.

I take a deep breath as I approach their room. "Come on, time for church."

"I'm sick. I'm not going."

"You're not sick. Get up. You're going."

"Why do I have to go to church?"

"Because we need to spend time with God."

"God's everywhere. That's what you said, so why do I have to go to church?"

"Because it's Sunday and we have to go and worship."

"I can pray here. I hate church. It's boring."

God, when I finally run out of arguments, I resort to the lowest sort of parental behavior. "Get moving. Until you're

18 you'll do what we say." So they finally drag out of the bedroom, carrying their beat-up tennis shoes, wearing the worst clothes they can find.

One evening our youngest was folding his clothes from the dryer. I said, "Look at that shirt. It's ripped and that black stain didn't come out. Why don't you just throw it away?" He clutched it to himself. "No, I'm saving it for church."

We try to keep calm as we drive to Mass. Ricky puts loud music on to "fix us." I grumble and turn it down. We find a pew and Rick and I wish with all our hearts we could sit on the other side of the aisle and pretend we're childless. But there we are, parents dressed nicely, next to kids who look like they're from a refugee camp. Along with their Sunday best clothes, they wear their Sunday best face—the sullen one that says, "My parents abuse me."

This one, our youngest (thank God), is wearing wrinkled shorts and a tattered tee shirt. He'd never be caught dead going to school like that. He has new church tactics. He cracks his knuckles, five at a time. I whisper in his ear, "You better stop or at the sign of peace, *darling*, I'll embarrass you so badly..." (I don't like the person he turns me into, but this is war.)

He forgets himself and almost smiles. He whispers back, "Okay, okay. I'll stop, but you better not kiss me."

I really get disturbed, God, when someone tells me that their family gathers around the table each night with their Bibles. They all take turns reading Scripture; then they share insights and talk over the events of the day. "Your whole family?" I ask, incredulously. They smile (smugly, I think) and answer, "Oh, yes."

"Even your teenagers?"

"Of course. We've been through the entire Bible three times now. And each night after we pray we all take a walk together." (They probably even take their holy dog, too!)

I can't take this, God. I really can't. The last time our kids were home at the same time I brought it up again. "The family that prays together stays together." I quoted. They disappeared.

Even at mealtime they want to rush things. "No, no. Don't let Mom pray," they say. "Anyone else. Anyone."

Help me to let go of this, God. They're yours! We've done the best we can. Recently, I heard a well-known theologian say we shouldn't push our kids about religion. We should just love them and trust the Holy Spirit to touch them at the right time. Now he tells me! Where was he all those Sundays when we had to badger our children to get out of bed and by the time we got to church everyone was so angry we didn't even know if we should go in!

Just a few more years and Rick and I can go alone and enjoy it. Help me to let our children's spiritual life be your concern, God. It's really too much for me.

Hysterectomy

OH, GOD, I DON'T like the news I received to-day. I went to a new gynecologist and he confirmed my darkest suspicions. I need major surgery, a hysterectomy, and now.

I can't believe two years have passed since that day I sat in another ob-gyn's office surrounded by glowing, pregnant women. How miserable I felt remembering the days when I was one of them. It was difficult to be in that type of waiting room for another reason. I had to see the doctor regarding the opposite end of the spectrum, the change of life years.

In relating that scene to a friend, she said, "They should have two waiting rooms. The door to one could be marked, 'Young Pregnant Women' and..." I interrupted, "the other could say, 'Old Menopausal Women.'"

Laughing about it helped, God, but what a struggle I've had to adjust to this time of life. I'm making progress, however, don't you think? Lately, I've even felt a certain excitement, an anticipation of the surprises you have in store for me in these later years.

The exam that day so long ago had revealed fibroid uterine tumors, a common occurrence in women my age. The doctor assured me they were not malignant and usually don't require treatment. However, if they were to grow and put pressure on other internal organs, then a hysterectomy would be needed.

The examination today revealed that one of the many tumors had indeed grown, to the size of a grapefruit, which was causing the prolonged bleeding and uncomfortable swelling of my abdomen.

I had no choice. I was headed for the hospital and six weeks away from a job I love.

Oh, God, I'm so frightened. Even after having three babies, I'm still wimpy about pain. The doctor was sensitive and understanding when I told him I have a low pain threshold. He made a notation, said he was glad I told him, and assured me he would monitor my pain medication carefully.

God, please don't let him forget. I don't want to make a complete fool of myself if the pain is too much. It's scheduled for next Wednesday. Only five days. God, please, please help me to let go of this awful fear.

Countdown

HOW'S NORM GOING TO get along without me, God? He depends on me. He asks me where things are and what's the status on this and that and so many other things that are only in my head. How can I train a temporary person in just a few days?

Six weeks, God. I can't leave my job for six weeks. It's mine. I've worked so hard to help develop procedures to make the office run more smoothly. I've established good relationships with the people Norm deals with. I'm important to his career, God. We're a team. How can I leave him?

I know, I know. I'm too possessive about my job. Why do people get that way? Maybe it's a way of being assured that we're needed. We have to believe that what we spend so much of our energy on is really important to the world.

Help me to let go of my job, God, at least for now. And please don't let the office be in shambles when I get back. But, God, I'm sorry—I'm only human—if you don't mind, please don't let it run too efficiently either.

I Could Die!

MY GOD, THE THOUGHT just hit me. I could die! I'm too young to die. I have too much unfinished business, too many projects I'm working on. My desk at home is cluttered. Rick would never be able to figure out my system of bookkeeping. I've paid the bills for 30 years!

My life has too many loose ends. My closets and drawers are a mess. I'm in the middle of a four-year Bible program. I'm growing my hair out. I've been asked to give the keynote speech at a convention. The keynote, God! I can't die until everything's finished. I want to die neat. That's not too much to ask, is it?

There's so much I haven't done. I want to take a philosophy class and read the great classics and watch Bogie in *Casablanca* one more time. I've never been on a roller coaster or seen a Broadway play. I want to find our relatives in Italy and hike the Grand Canyon and—oh, no, God—we never had our trip to Hawaii yet. Don't let me die!

I wonder if everyone feels this way before surgery. I know I'll be all right. I know it. Hysterectomies are one of the safest surgeries of all.

So why do I feel like I want to plan my funeral and write sentimental letters to all my loved ones? I can see them now, laughing and crying, showing their letters around. You know what I want them to say about me, Lord? I want them to say, "Judy was a woman who loved." That's what I want on my headstone, God. Do you think anyone will think of that?

I hope they don't just say funny things and tell stories on me (you know my friends). I don't mind that because I'm also a woman who laughs—I'd probably do the same to them—but most of all, God, I hope they remember how much I loved them.

I'm getting maudlin. Let Wednesday come quickly before I drive myself crazy. And please, God, help me to let go of this fear that I might die.

New Fertility

GOD, IF IT'S NOT one thing, it's another. Do you know what's upsetting me now? I'll never be able to have another baby. Funny, huh? As if I want to. But it's disturbing to think that the potential will be gone. The uterus that so lovingly carried and nourished our three babies is about to leave me forever.

After our youngest was born, I always wished I could be pregnant again. I didn't want to have any more babies, I just wanted to be pregnant. God, you know how I loved every moment of it, cherished every kick and hiccup and somersault from the tiny miracles growing in my body. Maybe it was because it took five years each time to become pregnant that I appreciated it so much.

Now they were going to take out even my ovaries and tubes, the tubes that were bent for most of my childbearing years, making it difficult to conceive. After all the tests and procedures and attention given to those tubes, now they were going to be cut out of me. This is too much, God. I have to think about this.

My subconscious is always one step ahead of my conscious mind, it seems. Last night I had an incredible dream. I dreamt that a crowd of people was assembled in a room waiting for an announcement a man was about to make. He stepped up to the platform and waited until the crowd grew silent. Then he said, "And she died due to natural causes." I looked around at all the people. They were stunned and one after another they burst into tears.

Here's what I wrote in my journal.

"I wasn't frightened by this dream, thinking I might die. I thought it might mean that the part of me that was fertile is dying a natural death. Its time has passed. But for the rest of my life my fertility will come in new ways. I feel that a new wave of creativity and spiritual power will be active in my life because I am a part of God and God is always creating."

Thank you for sending me that dream, God. I'm counting on my new fertility. Tomorrow's the day. I want to spend the rest of today meditating on your message. May it help me to let go of my reproductive organs, to allow them to die a natural death.

Wednesday Morning

IT'S TIME, GOD. There's no turning back. I think I'm ready. As frightened as I've been, this morning you surround me with a blanket of peace. I feel anesthetized already.

We drive to St. Joseph's Hospital, check in at Admitting, then wait in the lobby for a nurse to come and take me to my room. Rick holds my hand, looking concerned. "It's going to be all right, honey," he says.

I'm strangely calm. I wish I could have a cup of coffee.

The nurse finally comes, checks my ID bracelet, and asks if I need a wheelchair. I decline. Rick says he needs one. The nurse laughs and tells us a lot of husbands say that.

We walk and walk down a long corridor. She ushers us into another waiting room. I know I'm closer to the Operating Room now.

"I'm so scared," I tell my poor husband. He finds me some tissues. I didn't want to cry. I might lose control if I cry. He holds me close and comforts me and wipes my tears. A thought comes to me. I really could die. I try to tell my husband how much I love him. A nurse comes in before I can finish.

She takes me down another hallway into a room with two beds in it. She asks Rick to wait outside. I strip and put on a hospital gown. The nurse pulls tight-fitting white stockings over each foot on up to my knees, to prevent blood clots, she says. She's pleasant as she goes over all the same questions I've been asked numerous times.

"Do you smoke?"

"No."

"Are you allergic to any medicines?"

"No."

"Have you ever had diabetes, heart trouble, nervous disorders...?"

"No... no... no. I guess I'm an excellent candidate for surgery."

"You are."

I sigh. "I hope so."

I look at the ceiling as it races by me. Someone is pushing my bed down another long corridor into an elevator and down to x-ray. Rick is beside me chatting with whoever is pushing me.

An x-ray technician with curly hair comes out to the hallway and pulls my bed into another room. He says, "Can you sit up and move closer to the camera? We do a routine chest x-ray on all surgery patients."

"Sure."

He turns his back and I notice a sign that says, "If you are pregnant, be sure to tell the technician." I think I'll be funny and tell him I'm pregnant. Before I can get the words out he says to me, "Are you pregnant?" I shoot him a satirical look. He puts his hands up and laughs, "I have to ask. Honest. See the sign?"

The ceiling was racing past me again. We stop before ominous double doors marked "Operating Room." A young man dressed in blue comes out, checks my ID bracelet, puts a white cap on my head, and tells Rick this is where he has to leave me.

Rick kisses me. "I know you'll be fine. I love you."

The huge doors stand open. There was so much I wanted to say to my husband but I knew he already knew it. All that came out was, "Don't forget I want a cup of coffee as soon as I'm awake."

More waiting. An hour in another hallway. "I'm sorry," someone says. "It's crazy in here today. We're running behind schedule."

I try to doze. Someone gives me a shot. Then the ceiling moves again and I am in the OR. They lift me onto another bed. A large, bright lamp is above me.

Masked nurses and doctors are busy putting things on me and working with equipment and instruments. They chat with me and I hear myself quietly respond. Most of the time I keep my eyes closed. I don't want to know what they're doing.

Earlier in the morning I had prayed, "Help me to do this well, God. Help me to be brave. Tell me to breathe deeply and please tell me you love me. Remind me that your Word says that I could walk through fire and not be burned, and raging waters and not drown and that you would never, never leave me. Sing my favorite song to me. 'Be not afraid. I go before you always. Come, follow me and I will give you rest.'"

Someone said, "Judy, I'm going to put you to sleep now."

Help me, God, to let go and trust you with my life.

Thank God, It's Over

GOD, THANK YOU, thank you, that it's over. I'm home now. I didn't die. Thank you for helping me to let go and trust you with my very life.

The first 24 hours were rough but you helped me. I didn't lose control and was able to manage the pain much better than I expected. I think I did it well. I really think I did!

You are so good to me, God. No cancer, no complications, no infections. The hospital staff treated me so kindly. Many of the nurses had gone through the same operation so they understood the awful gas pains, the discomfort, and the tears. They encouraged me and told me in a few days I would feel much better. They were right, God.

Once in the middle of the night I thought I had a bona-fide hallucination. A young nurse was trying to find my vein to start an IV. Twice she failed and splattered blood on my clean, white sheet. She was trying a third time and I was about to tell her to forget it when a handsome young doctor poked his head around the curtain. He was tall and muscular and had longish curly, brown hair. He was dressed in surgical blues and had a stethoscope around his neck. He said something to the nurse and left the room.

"Is he a doctor?" I asked.

She nodded yes. She was a bit shaken by him as evidenced by her third fail at attempting to find a vein. "Why don't you give this thing up? That hurts... Are you sure he's a doctor? He looks like someone from the soaps." He came around the corner again and asked the nurse about another patient, then left.

"He looks like Prince Charming," I said. "Is there a white horse in the hallway?"

She sighed. "I know. I never saw him before but I've heard about him. That's Dr. Farello. You wouldn't happen to know if he's married, would you?"

"How would I know? I just got here. Do you want me to find out for you?"

She smiled. "Would you?"

"I will if you'll stop sticking me."

The next morning Prince Charming appeared at my bedside. "I'm Dr. Farello. I'm a resident here, filling in today for Dr. Scott who assisted your gynecologist in surgery. How are you doing?"

"Oh, a little uncomfortable, but not as awful as I expected." I wanted to say, "You know, I don't always look this bad. You should see me when I'm all dressed up in the morning for work." Instead I reached my hand up to try to smooth my messy hair only to realize I was finally attached to the IV bottle and couldn't move very far. I decided it was futile. I was a mess and that was that.

"Let me hear you breathe. Can you sit up?"

"Sure. I think."

"Good. Sounds good."

I felt a little bold and a little silly. Must have been the pain medication. What the heck, I thought. I'll never see him again. I said, "I think you're an imposter."

"An imposter?"

"Yea. I think you're a soap opera doctor."

He loved it. "Sure. Well, really I'm a guy from house-keeping who stole this blue uniform so I could play doctor."

"Are you married?" (I promised Karen I would ask.)

"Yes, I am. And quite happy, as a matter of fact, for 11 years."

"That's nice."

"Uh... what character do you think I am on the soaps?"

"I don't know. I never watch them any more."

We had a pleasant exchange before he left. "I probably won't see you any more. Dr. Scott will be back. Hope you feel better soon."

"Thanks. See you on General Hospital."

Well, God, I feel better. I'm sorry, but it's just so good to know I'm still a woman!

When Do You
Get Your Life Back?

THE FIRST WEEK HOME when I was spending most of my time resting on the couch, Valerie looked at me so pitifully and said, "When do you get your life back, Mom?"

I'm ready to get my life back now, God. Three weeks at home and I'm antsy. I want to go back to work. My mind says I'm ready but my body doesn't seem to be taking orders from my mind any more. I tire easily and cry easily and I don't like it at all. God, please help me to be patient while I heal.

I wasn't prepared for the way I felt after surgery—fragile, vulnerable, like suddenly I'm made of glass. Especially in the hospital, God, I knew I was completely at your mercy. And even though I'm making an excellent recovery, some part of me feels like I've never before been so close to death. It's hard to really grasp this feeling. It flirts around my consciousness, emerging and sinking as soon as it's noticed.

I didn't realize that major surgery could deal such a tremendous psychic blow. Help me to accept it and to be patient while my body, mind, and spirit heal. It doesn't happen so quickly, I'm discovering. But I know it's happening.

How wonderful you have made us, dearest God. In a way that I don't fully understand, I know I am programmed for health. Like a flower reaching for the sun, every part of me reaches for you, God, and in you there is wholeness.

God, will I be stronger on every level now? I've heard it said that once a broken bone has mended, it becomes stronger than before. Often people who have been crushed and broken by life turn into the most compassionate, gentle souls. And therein lies their strength.

What power there is in gentleness. Tremendous waves of love can flow through "wounded healers." "I solemnly assure you, unless the grain of wheat falls to the earth and dies, it remains just a grain of wheat. But if it dies, it produces much fruit." (John 12:24)

Help me to be patient, God, as you give me my "new" life back. Please knit me together stronger and gentler than before, that I may be one of your wounded healers.

Mutt and Jeff

I JUST CAN'T RECKON with time, God. No matter how much I try, it mystifies me. I opened a closet door today and there were the two plastic bags again, holding a first communion dress and a wedding gown, still standing side by side, like Mutt and Jeff. It all came back to me.

Could it possibly have been five years since our oldest daughter's wedding? How well I remembered the preparation, the anxiety, the nervous little spats, before it all miraculously came together at the last minute.

Everything was beautiful and René never looked happier as she moved gracefully down the aisle, escorted by her nervous father.

The day went too fast and we stumbled into the house at midnight. Rick's tux was wrinkled and he had unbuttoned his bow tie, which was dangling down one side. My long, peach dress was a mess. "My feet are killing me," I said. I plopped down on the couch. "Oh, I'm half dead."

Rick moaned. "I'm all dead. Move over. I don't have enough strength to fall all the way to the floor."

"What a day. I can't believe it worked out so well. Just think, hon, you're a father-in-law. It was worth all the grief, wasn't it?"

"I don't know. It cost us a fortune. We'll be paying for

years. So help me, if the other two get an idea like this, you and I are going to take the ladder and the money we offered René."

"Hmmm, that sounds like an interesting idea. We could run away from home and they could call us when it's all over. Where could we go? Hawaii? The Bahamas? Rick... Rick. Go to bed. You're snoring."

The next day I walked into our daughter's empty room. I remembered teasing her when she and Terry moved everything into their new apartment. "You know, you never did clean your room, René. Aren't you ashamed? I've been telling you for years to clean it and all you did was move your messy room into your messy car and drive off."

"That's okay, Mom. Now it's in my messy apartment, just as it should be."

I never could put a guilt trip on that kid, God. You know I tried.

I smiled as I looked around her room. Well, it was finally clean. Just a rainbow poster still hanging on the wall. My rainbow girl.

I opened her closet door to take a look at the wedding gown that cost a fortune. It was hanging crooked, the train wrinkled and dirt stained where her Dad had accidentally stepped on it at the altar. The long veil draped down elegantly nearly to the floor.

I looked to the end of the closet to see if she had forgotten anything. After all, I was laying claim to this room. At the far end of the closet I noticed one lone, short, plastic bag. It looked vaguely familiar. I slid the bag up next to the wedding gown. A slight shiver went down my spine when I remembered it was René's first communion dress.

I removed the plastic bag and let it fall to the floor. The tiny communion dress and veil now hung next to the long wedding gown and veil—both had held the same delicate body.

The image before me was too powerful. I sat down on the floor feeling as empty as the room. Memories flooded me as I realized my little girl was gone.

Flashes of our daughter's childhood and vivid pictures of me as a young mother clicked in rapid succession in my mind, my own private slide show. What was I crying about? Was it my little girl leaving or my lost youth?

Sitting cross-legged on my daughter's bedroom floor, looking at the two white dresses, I heard in my mind just as clearly as I had heard it 22 years before. After five years of trying to have a baby, the doctor finally said, "Judy, this time the tests are positive. You're really pregnant."

The pictures kept coming. "Look, Rick. Hurry. René just took her first step." Tears rolled down my face. I remembered her little voice say, "Mom, I'm really mad. Laura said I was a Catholic and I yelled at her and told her I was an Es-way!"

I remembered the autumn day when we were all in the front yard. Rick had just raked a huge pile of crisp, brightly colored leaves to the side. He went to get the trash bag and said, "Now, René, don't you dare jump into those leaves." What an invitation for a seven year old! As soon as his back was turned, I saw her fly through the air and land kerplunk in the delicious pile of leaves. (I almost did it myself!)

As she was crawling out, she squealed with delight and threw a handful of leaves in the air. Then she saw her Dad coming. She wiped the smile off her face, looked sheepish, and said sincerely, "The devil made me do it....Honest, Daddy."

More scenes came to my mind. "Mom, watch me twirl around in my communion dress...." "I know you're going to say I'm too young, Mom, but everyone in seventh grade has a boyfriend." "Mom, help me try on my wedding gown, will you?"

The ring of the phone startled me. It was our daughter

calling from her honeymoon in California. "Mom, just wanted to tell you we're here safe and sound and thank you and Dad for everything. Mom, I'm so happy... Why are you crying?"

"Because. You just made your first communion."

"Huh?"

"Your first communion dress. It's still in your closet next to your wedding gown."

"Sooo?"

"Well, you just made your first communion yesterday and now you're grown up and married and I don't know how it all happened."

"Oh, Mom... you are really such a Mom!"

That was five years ago and now she's a Mom, too, with three precious little girls of her own. And God, time continues to baffle and elude me. Her little girls and my little girls confuse me because somehow they cross over each other in time. I know it sounds crazy, but do you know what I mean?

Words...Words...Words...

GOD, SOMETIMES I WISH I lived before the printing press was invented. The information age can be so stressful.

My love affair with books can be injurious to my mental health. There's so much I want to learn, so much wisdom there just for the taking, if only a person had enough hours in the day.

Except for being a "newsaholic," I've long since let go of television in order to read more and it's still not enough. But God, right now my brain is so tired and overloaded that I don't care if I ever read another thing.

There's a stack of magazines piling up faster than I can get to them. There's books in every room in the house, in various stages of completion. I pick one up and feel like I have to start over because I've lost the gist of it after so long. I've pledged time and again not to start reading another book until I've finished the one I'm reading. But something comes along that interests me and I can't wait to get into it.

Then there's the stack of "special" books that I'm intent on reading again, the ones that changed my life.

And why do I keep subscribing to so many things? They mount up so fast that the stack seems to take on a menacing life. It should be illegal to publish anything weekly! Quarterly or annually should be the only thing allowed. Of course, then it would be four volumes each time and I'd be in the same boat. I just can't win.

Help me with this madness, God. Please direct my learning. Show me what you want me to read and take away my interest in the things that are not in your plan. I need your Holy Spirit to be my private tutor and to draw me a personalized curriculum—one that I can live with.

White Knuckles

I HAVE SO MANY fears, God. Fear of flying, fear of the night, fear of being alone. Even fear of admitting I have so many fears. I think if I admit to them they'll somehow take over my life. Is there any hope for me?

And yet, you've helped me so much, God. Thank you for giving me the courage to start flying again after many years. The fear is not completely gone but at least my knuckles aren't white any more. However, I'd be a lot more comfortable if they just wouldn't say things like "Terminal 2, Last Call, and Final Approach."

Help me to trust you more, God. Your Word says that you know our comings and goings, when we sit and when we stand. When I'm on a plane, I secretly wonder if you also know our goings up and our comings down. You know I'm just being silly, God.

And I'm still afraid of being alone at night. I lock doors and check windows and feel totally ashamed that I find it so difficult to trust you when the sun goes down.

I make sure our little dog, PJ, is close beside me. He barks ferociously at the slightest sound. I rationalize that you use him to help make me feel safe, but I hope you don't notice how much trust I'm placing in a little pint-sized pooch.

Please stay close to me, God, and let me feel it. Please fill our house with a strong sense of your presence always, especially during the night.

African Violets and People

GOD, HOW WONDERFUL IT is when I'm able to truly live in the present moment. Help me to let go more quickly of thoughts and conversations, feelings and moods. I know reflection is good but I'm a chronic lingerer, taking too long and expending too much energy on every experience. It wearies me, God.

Today I sat in my prayer room—that wonderful room where I think and pray and write—our room, God. I sat perfectly still and focused on the African violets near the window that give me so much pleasure. I tried to blot everything out, to live fully in the present moment. The violets began to teach me about life.

The deep, purple flowers on one plant were gorgeous. Most of the leaves were thick and green, but one leaf drooped. I would have to pinch it off to keep the plant healthy.

Another was unusual with delicate, paper-thin, pale pink flowers. It reminded me of people who are sensitive and shy, but flourish when given the proper care and understanding.

One plant had a single flower in bloom and the whole plant looked slightly deformed. It hadn't formed in the usual manner, but had leaves going off every which way. But somehow I loved that plant. It seemed to have had quite a struggle to yield that one flower. It was like some people I know who hear their own music and march to a different beat.

One plant had no flowers in bloom at the moment but was loaded with buds that would all blossom very soon if only I water it, give it just the right amount of light—not too much and not too little—and send it warm vibrations. I know it will reward me in due time. I thought of all the areas of my life I've been working on, a little at a time. If I just persevere, perhaps they might all bloom overnight.

And one plant was spectacular—large, in full bloom. Deep lavender velvety flowers seemed to dance everywhere. Every strong, green leaf was perfect. The entire plant was shaped beautifully. It was in its prime.

Were you speaking to me about different people, God? Or was it more about different parts of myself. Will the deformed parts of my personality dare to present themselves to my conscious mind? And if they do, will I love them or find them utterly distasteful?

How I want to be like the perfect violet, in full bloom, flowers bouncing everywhere. But perhaps I have to be like every one of the other violets first, God, and trust that you will provide what I need at each stage of my development.

I've learned so much today by letting go and emptying my mind so I could see—really see—what is right before my eyes. Help me to do this more often so you can teach me. And, God, thank you for creating flowers.

Happy House

WE HAVE TO MOVE, God, and I want to, but how will I ever be able to let go of this house? It's not as if we've lived here forever. It's only been eight years, but they were wonderful years.

We have no choice. The drive to work is wearing me down. An hour each way in heavy traffic leaves me exhausted at night. We've put off moving because we love this house but lately it seems my life is out of control. We have to do something to make things more manageable.

I wish we could just pick the house up and move it across town. It's been a happy house. I think people feel it when they walk in the front door. Lots of welcome hugs have taken place in the entry way. I could cry remembering all the beautiful people that came through that door.

Just last year, more than 40 friends were here to surprise Rick on his 50th birthday. I'll never forget the look on his face when I opened the door to greet him. The lights came on and a shout rang out, "Happy Birthday." His mouth dropped open and he was so stunned I thought he was going to fall over.

And then there were all the Sundays we had guests over for Rick's famous pasta. The house smelled of sauce and garlic and people were happy. The kids were always bringing friends home for dinner and often to stay the night. It was like Grand Central Station and we loved it, well at least most of the time.

One morning I came out to start the coffee and found a teenage boy, a complete stranger, sound asleep on the living room couch. I tiptoed past him into René's bedroom. "Who's that on the couch?" I asked her. "I sure hope you know him."

"That's my friend, Mark, Mom. He's having a little problem at home. I told him he could stay here for a few days. I knew you'd say okay."

Mark stayed for three weeks!

How I love our patio. I can still hear the music, laughter, and stimulating conversations that went late into the warm, Arizona nights. Lois, our nun friend, who loved to clown, would show up at odd times. She'd find us out on the patio and make her entrance tap dancing and singing, or doing a soft shoe.

And Father Memo, the Redemptorist missionary who adopted us for his family, made this patio sing with laughter with his hilarious stories told in different dialects. When he wasn't being zany and making us roar, he was wooing us, softly strumming his guitar and singing beautiful songs.

And God, there was so much talk about you in this house. So many conversations that touched our souls, sweet spiritual friendship with people who love you. Your presence in this house is what made it a happy house.

Even when there were fights, you taught us how to forgive. We matured in this house. We learned how to give and take, and that loving relationships can be a source of spiritual power.

God, this house is full of vibrations and energies from all that was lived here. Bless the new people, the lucky people, who will now live in this house. And may our new house be filled with the same ambience. It couldn't possibly be any other way, now could it, because you're moving with us, aren't you, God?